Pet
Tales

Copyright Notices

Legal Notices

Pet Tales

". . . Ask the animals and they will teach you,

Or the birds of the air, and they will tell you."

Job 12:7

For Ailia, Emily, Ivy, Will and Anna

Merry Christmas, 2013

Love, Grandma Bliss

Contents

Introduction

"How are your cats, Grandma?" Emily would ask twice a week on our long distance phone calls. I, Grandma, live in Illinois. Emily lives in California.

In an attempt to communicate with her, her sisters and cousins, this book has evolved. In an effort to paint a picture for my grandchildren of animals I've loved, animals that have made me giggle and animals that have spoken to me, this has been written. Two other stories, a few poems and bits of whimsy developed as I was writing about my pets.

So here, Emily, are stories of my cats, dogs, a rabbit or two and a little more.

Maggie and Maya

"Hey, Grandma. How are your cats?" Emily asked. Grandpa Bliss and I have two feral calico cats, one found in the woods and one found left in an empty apartment building. They look alike, but they are different.

When we first saw Maggie, the woods cat, she was climbing up a window screen. Curious, easily startled, very full of energy, we think she might be part raccoon.

MONDAY

On Monday, I went about my household chores, humming under my breath and talking to my friend, Maggie. She helped me make the bed, hiding in turn under each layer of sheets and blankets. I put the clean towels into the linen closet. Maggie followed and made note of "dark space, soft towels." Of course, I found Maggie in there later and had to be careful not to close the door on her.

Next, I found her napping in the toilet, lying on the porcelain as if on the beach by the ocean.

After washing her paws, I had lunch with Maggie and tried to read the paper. She would have none of that. She would sit on the paper and stare at me with big eyes as I chewed my food. Then I cleared the dishes off the table, put the food away, and washed the dishes. After that, curiously the newspaper was free again. So I read a couple more articles.

I heard a soft "mew." Where was Maggie? I checked the linen closet. No Maggie. I checked the bed. No Maggie. She wasn't in the toilet. I went into the utility room and checked behind the washer and dryer and furnace. No Maggie. I retraced my steps. The last time I saw her was at lunch. I remember I cleaned up lunch, put the dirty plate in the sink, put the food back in the refrigerator. I opened the refrigerator door and there sat Maggie on top of the ham and cheese! Oh! There were so many hugs and kisses before she settled next to me for a much needed nap. Good grief!

TUESDAY

On Tuesday, Maggie was following me around again. I was putting food away and being careful not to let Maggie in the refrigerator, making sure the burners on the stove were turned off, straightening the newspaper, and turning to clear the counter, when PLOP! Oatmeal and milk were splashing out of a bowl. Maggie had jumped from the floor unto the counter, landing in the middle of a bowl of oatmeal! She liked food! She also had her first bath! She didn't like that as much.

All plants were relocated to higher and higher shelves. Maggie would eat them, get sick all over the house, and then return to eat some more.

After eating dinner and snacks, Maggie showed us her contentment and love. At night she cuddled with me on the couch for a few minutes. Then she climbed on the back of the couch and rearranged my hair.

WEDNESDAY

Maggie has a sloppy heart filled with love. She likes her house, her food, being petted, and kisses. She likes playing catch. Her little balls, like furry mice, roll across the floor.

She became a house cat. The outdoors beckoned to her only on the mildest and sunniest of days, a rarity in the Chicago area.

On Wednesday, Maggie read the newspaper with me. "Love me," she said. "Let me lean on you. Kiss. Kiss. Nip." She always ended her love sessions with a slight nip. Her mother must have been stern. The nips, I've decided, are a kind of love pat. No amount of protesting on our parts have stopped it, but she is a bit gentler now. "Kiss. Kiss. Nip. Give me the pen. Give me the paper. Love. Love. Nip." Maggie hugged my ankle when I got up to leave. I looked at Maggie as I was dragging my foot and her across the floor, and said, "You need a friend!"

THURSDAY, FRIDAY, AND SATURDAY

So, we got Maya.

She was found in an empty apartment building. She was sick. She was hungry. She was afraid of the world and she was afraid of men. Maya was feral and she had her left ear tattooed after she was caught and spayed. Maya was pretty and had markings similar to Maggie. Not thinking all that clearly, I brought her home to be a friend for Maggie.

Because Maya was new and because she was sick, we gave her a room of her own at first. We fed her and petted her and tried to let her get to know us and feel safe. We gave her medicine and saw her slowly start to feel better.

Maggie took up a sentry position outside the door. "What's going on in there?" she wanted to know. The stand-off lasted a few days. I'm not sure who put her paw under the door first, but one did, and the other cat responded. That's how Maggie and Maya got to know one another.

SUNDAY

I hoped the cats would be friends, but Maggie wasn't happy about sharing her people. If Maya tried to play "chase the ball," Maggie swatted it away or sulked. If Maya got petted, Maggie stalked away. "What do we need another cat for anyway?" she wanted to know.

On Sunday, Maggie and Maya had a fight and it got loud. Maya screamed. Maggie chased her, backing her into a corner and hissing. Then the hitting and biting began. That's when I had to break the fight up. Maya came shaking at my feet. Maggie, nervously crouched, was ready to run at and pounce on

Maya. Luckily, the cats have only so much energy. Their fight lasted a few minutes and then they crept into opposite corners of the house and took a nap.

I have tried to talk to the cats about their feelings and about each other. The talks usually don't go very well. "What are you saying cat?" I ask.

"I want to be petted, but my stomach hurts."

"That might be because you ate the leaves off the plant again."

"I want to be petted, but the other cat is bothering me...Okay. I did want to be petted, but that's enough, and that's why I'm nipping you."

"I don't want a treat. I want regular food. NOW!"

"I don't want you to know how much I need you."

And, then she – either one of the shes – will purr, from the bottom of her back toes. She will purr like a gravel grinder.

THE NEXT MONDAY

Grandpa Bliss leapt out of bed. He threw off his comforter. He ripped off his top sheet. "Aaargh!" he shouted. "Something ran over my back and woke me up!"

He stomped out of the bedroom, closed the door and went into the living room. He tried to sleep on the couch.

"Was it one of the cats jumping on the bed?" I asked. "Was it a tail brushing your back?"

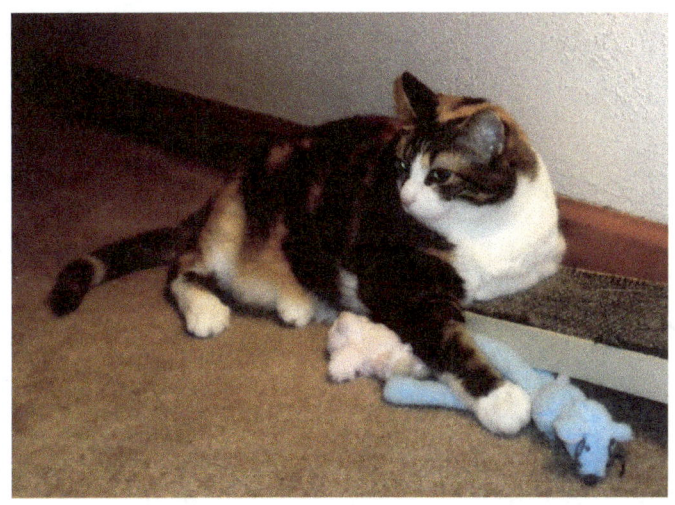

"No. It was a mouse or a hamster," Grandpa groused.

"A mouse or a hamster? How can that be?" I asked. "We have two cats who would never allow a mouse or a hamster into the bedroom."

Maya rarely moves unless there is a sunbeam rolling across the floor. She'll chase the sunbeam and she'll be very fast. She'd probably chase a mouse or a hamster, and she'd be very fast.

Maggie would definitely chase a mouse or a hamster. She would want it to play with her.

"Could it have been a bug? Could it have been a part of a dream?" I persisted.

"I don't know, but I'm going to search every corner of that room. I'm going to find the critter that woke me up!" Grandpa said as he lay back on the couch.

Then, out of the corner of my eye, I saw Maggie creep out of the bedroom…

THE NEXT TUESDAY

Maya watches her people and Maggie. She looks for ways to join in peacefully. When it seems calm, she will play and amuse herself.

On the next Tuesday, I slept in. Maya waited for me to wake up. She lay near my head and sent thought waves to me. "Get up. Get up. Maggie is hungry." So, Maya made sure that breakfast got served and another day was begun.

Maya saw me playing catch with Maggie, and she wanted to play too. Seeing her chance, Maya batted a crinkly ball at Maggie. Maggie looked at the ball, mumbled under her breath, and walked away. Maya shrugged it off and went to chase Maggie's shadow as sunbeams crossed the floor.

Maya seems to have accepted Maggie's moods, and she tries to make the best of it. Maggie, because she is still very much loved and because Maya lets her be boss, is beginning to accept Maya into her life.

TODAY

Maya still chases sunbeams and tries to engage Maggie in play.

Grandpa Bliss is still wary of creatures in his bedroom, but he has put up a new scratching post by the window. He has also cleaned that window.

The cats still fight sometimes, but they also get along better at other times. They have learned to talk and to listen to each other some of the time.

The cats still like to play the "paws under the door" game.

Maggie is still clingy, but some of our happiest times are spent talking and cuddling each other. She still does not like my hair and tries to rearrange it.

So, Emily, I think my cats are doing okay. What do you think?

Easter, 2012

Maggie Cat was very bad
We think she's gone totally mad
She knocked my glasses off the table
Chewed them up as much as able
Then she ate my Easter flowers
And scattered them all over the foyer
She attacked the jelly beans, unseen
She left a very messy scene

And who does she try to blame?
The other cat, Maya!
Maya aghast
Said this is the last!
Maya woke me from my sleep
With one tiny, teeny peep
There is no Easter joy with Maggie
She is a one-cat cat-astrophe!

Maggie, this is not even funny
Now she's blaming the Easter bunny!

Phyllis the Flamingo

Once upon a time there was a flamingo named Phyllis who wandered off from her family.

"I'm lost! Oh no! Where am I? Where are all the others?"

Phyllis Flamingo lived with her mother, her father, her grandmother, 12 brothers, 16

sisters, and all kinds of aunts, uncles and cousins at the Los Angeles Zoo. She was thinking about what her cousin had said about another cousin, when a hot pink balloon floated by and she followed it. All of a sudden, she realized she wasn't with her family anymore. Where was she? Where was her family? "How do I find my way home?"

As Phyllis walked up the path still chasing the balloon, she ran into a boy with a round face, straw colored hair and freckles.

"Oooh!" the boy said. "What a pretty colored bird! I want a feather!" Rudely, he reached out and plucked a feather from her upper back.

"Ouch!" yelled Phyllis. She ran away from the boy to the first display off the main path.

She found herself with the meerkats. This caused quite a stir in the meerkat's home because they are afraid of big birds. Large birds were known to swoop down on meerkat families and carry off their young.

Phyllis asked, "Can I stay with you for a while? I'm lost and not sure where home is. If I stay on the path a bratty kid will pluck out my feathers!"

The meerkats were still wary of the big, pink bird. But, watching Phyllis, they realized she meant them no harm, would probably not eat them, and was truly lost and in some trouble.

Phyllis saw that the meerkats lived in a fairly large group and they chattered a lot between themselves. It gave Phyllis some comfort because this was like a flamingo family. But, the meerkats were not feathered and they were not pink.

"Would you like a snack?" one of the meerkats asked her. "We have some small insects here."

"No, thank you," Phyllis said. Insects would not sate the hunger she felt. Flamingos did not eat insects. They ate small fish and shrimp. Besides, the longing she felt was for her home, not food. "I have to be on my way," she said. "Thank you for letting me rest here a moment."

"Good luck to you. The giraffes are down the path. They can see further than we can. Perhaps they can help you find your home," the meerkats offered helpfully.

Following the meerkat's directions and avoiding the children on the path, Phyllis found the giraffe's display. It was a large area full of sand and tall trees with few leaves on the top. The grass had been eaten long ago.

"Can you help me?" Phyllis asked the giraffes. I'm lost and I'm not sure where my family is."

"Come here, little sister. Rest a while. I'm not sure where your family is. Let's see..." Jerome Giraffe looked up and down the path and craned his neck to look around the corners of the path, but he didn't see a flock of flamingos. He plucked a leaf from the nearest tree, chewed his cud, and thought a moment, maybe two moments, because giraffes took their time about things.

"We could be related," he said. We both have long necks and long legs. You can stay here a while. Would you like to snack on a leaf?"

"No thank you. I really need to find my family," Phyllis said.

"Perhaps the elephants can help you. They are very smart and they have long memories. Maybe they remember seeing your family and know where they are located in the zoo," Jerome said.

"That would be very helpful. Thank you, Jerome Giraffe." Phyllis again took a walk down the path. She walked carefully along the edge of the path avoiding children and golf carts. She tried to hide behind bushes, but it was hard because she was so pink and it showed against the green grass and bushes.

Phyllis soon found the elephants. A couple were Asian elephants that had retired from a circus. They were playing with huge balls that were props from the circus.

"Hi, Flamingo," the two elephants greeted her when they noticed her watching them. "Would you like to try balancing on the circus ball?"

Thinking of her long, skinny legs on the moving ball, Phyllis backed away from the idea. "No. Thank you though. I'm lost and looking for my family. The giraffes thought you might know where to find them."

"Hmm," said the largest elephant. "I remember a flock of them on the edge of a body of water. I think it was a ways back, past the giraffe's home."

Phyllis realized she would have to do some back tracking.

"Would you like something to eat before you set off down the path again?" one elephant asked. "We have some fruit."

Phyllis was starting to feel hungry, but she didn't eat fruit. "No, thank you. You've been helpful, but if I go now, maybe I'll find my family by dinner time."

"Good luck, Flamingo," the two elephants said together. Then the biggest one said, "Try and find that body of water."

Phyllis again walked down the path, past the giraffes, past a group of school children and past the meerkats. She came to a small body of water with some fish in it. Maybe this was it, but it didn't quite look right.

Then she saw the crocodile! It was very big and had very big teeth! This was not right! This was not right for sure!

Shaken and disturbed, Phyllis ran back to the path. A little girl named Ivy walked up behind her. "Excuse me, Flamingo," she said.

Phyllis was so startled she shrieked and jumped a foot! "Please don't touch me. Please don't pluck my feathers," said Phyllis.

"I'm not going to do that," said Ivy. Then she asked, "Are you lost? If you are, maybe I can help. I live a few blocks from here and know the zoo pretty well."

"I am. I can't find my family," she told the little girl.

"Well, I just saw your family and I think they are looking for you," Ivy said.

"Where are they?" Phyllis asked.

Ivy said, "Across the path and down a ways. Can you hear them? They are talking up a storm! I'll take you to them and keep other children away from you."

"Oh. Thank you!" said Phyllis. She followed the little girl across the path and to the left. There they were! Her big, huge chatty family! "Mother. Father. I found you! I was lost. I'm so glad I found you! Thanks to Ivy. She helped me find my way home!"

"You're just in time for dinner," said her mother.

To her brothers and sisters, Phyllis said, "I met the meerkats, the giraffes, the elephants and a crocodile. Be careful of children because they might pluck your feathers. But not all children. Some are helpful and kind, like Ivy, and will help you find your way home if you're lost. It is so good to be home!"

Geese

The geese have taught me
There are two ways to get into the water.
Your choice.

The first way is to tiptoe over the flat rocks
Lifting billowing tutu tail feathers
And gracefully slide into the water.
No fuss. No muss.
With dignity, glide through the water.

The second way is to hold back,
Wait impatiently,
Then, with much honking and flapping of wings
Fly over the serene sisters,
Fly to the far end of the lake
And crash in, just before hitting land,
Splattering water,
Scattering dragonflies and lily pads.

There are two ways to go through your life.
Your choice.

Summer Duet

It's hot. It's humid.
The air hangs still.
Nothing moves.
But, hush.
I am an honored
Audience of one.

An unseen bird offers
Two sweet tweets
Answered by another
A low ta ta ta ta
Two different species
Hiding in full green trees
Passing the time
Singing a summer duet.
Tweet. Tweet.
Ta Ta Ta Ta.
The air is less hot, less humid.
It sings

Blessing

I was standing, staring into the distance.

I felt a fluttering of wings

Brush against my cheek.

A butterfly?

No. A hummingbird!

A tiny, yet fat, grey hummingbird

Earnestly flying to the purple hosta flowers.

It was surprised to see me

But, it shook the shock off

And flew to the coneflowers,

Leaving me standing,

Smiling

And counting

My many blessings.

Ralph and Olaf

Do you remember Ralph, Ailia? You met him when you were very young. The storms of life, betrayal, fire and misunderstandings brought the big, white cat to my door. It was one of the luckiest days of my life.

His name was Ralph. Everyone knew that because he said, "I'm Ralph," clear as the sunniest of days. One time I sat in front of him and said, "Hi honey." He looked me in the eye, put his right paw on my knee and said, "I'm Ralph." And, so he was.

I also had a small, white, dwarf rabbit. He was given the name, Olaf, a big name to bulk up his tiny frame. He was larger than a mouse and smaller than a rat. I worried about whether the new cat would harm him.

Your mom and dad were visiting on the day we introduced Ralph to Olaf. Ralph was sitting regally on the back of the couch. He knew something was up as we were moving furniture and planning the best way to save the rabbit if Ralph decided to attack him. But, introductions had to be made since they would be living together. Ralph sat and waited and watched his people scurry around.

We brought out Olaf. Ralph's ears shot up. His eyes opened wide. His tail quivered. He started to drool. We feared he was thinking, "lunch." Ralph stared, alert.

The snow colored Olaf hopped around, unaware of the cat. It was clear he was thinking something like, "Oh goody. New things to explore. New things to chew."

Ralph pounced!

In unison we all shouted, "No!" Ralph looked around, startled. He had forgotten he had an audience.

Olaf pooped on the floor. I picked Olaf up and petted him. I let Ralph sniff him. "Bunnies are our friends," I told Ralph.

Ralph looked like he wasn't sure about that. But if his people liked the bunny, he had better leave the bunny alone. It was better than having everyone shout at him.

For years afterwards we would bring Ralph little toy mice to play with. He would play with the brown ones, the gray ones and the black ones. But he would never play with the white ones.

Olaf's reaction to Ralph was pure, deep and strong. He was in LOVE! Oh, how he loved Ralph! Olaf looked at the big, white fluffy cat, so like his own white, fluffy self and he thought, "LOVE!"

Olaf set out to prove his love to Ralph. He followed Ralph everywhere. If Ralph jumped on the couch, Olaf jumped on the couch. If Ralph walked on the back of the couch, Olaf jumped on the back of the couch, trying to match the cat's stride. If Ralph jumped on the window sill, Olaf, well, Olaf couldn't jump that high. He just sat below and stared longingly at Ralph, the object of his affection.

Ralph seemed to understand. Even though this tiny rabbit was always under foot, Ralph was patient, kind and gentle with him.

Everyone knows that rabbits don't talk. But when Ralph purred, Olaf tried to copy him with a low growl. I know it is hard to believe, but the rabbit tried to purr! He loved

Ralph. He would prove it by becoming like Ralph, the most cat-like rabbit you ever saw!

As much as Olaf tried to be a cat, Ralph tried to be human. He looked for ways to be helpful. He spent a lot of time policing the patio window and he kept tabs on the comings and goings of all people, dogs, birds and insects. He always greeted people who came in the front door. Every morning when the newspaper came, Ralph woke me up to let me know.

When I returned to the house from work or errands, I would greet Ralph and ask him, "any calls?" He answered by mewing once or twice for each call. One time I got home and Ralph was very excited, very talkative.

He paced up and down until I asked, "calls?" I had three phone calls! He took his duties very seriously, but that may have been a bit too much.

Ralph had a favorite easy chair he would slouch in when we watched TV at night. He never learned how to use the TV remote. He did, however, learn quite a few words in the English language. He tried to talk.

Do you remember that Ailia? Ralph learned a lot of human words. "Ma" and "R" were what he called me and Art. He'd greet us and others with "hi." One day I said, "Hi Ralph. How are you?" He answered, "I'm ine." He meant "I'm fine." That took my breath away and had me thinking of little else that night.

Ralph told me when he was hungry. Well, he was always hungry. But "eat" was another word he knew. His favorite "play" was a stick with feathers at the end.

"Ni ni" was the bed we slept in. One time we moved. The movers met with protest when they packed up the "ni ni" and started to move it.

"Mgr" meant "I'm mad at you" or "you moved too fast and scared me." That's when Ralph would mumble under his breath and walk stiffly away.

One day I asked Ralph, "What would you like me to tell people? What would you like me to tell my grandchildren?" He said four things:

1.   "Tell them that love is everything. Even if it's only the love of little, white bunnies.

2.   Tell them love lasts forever.

3.   Tell them as long as there's plenty of food, everything will be okay.

4.   And, tell them we cats understand our people much more than you think we do."

Can you remember that Ailia?

Yes, I was very lucky when Ralph came to live with me. He taught me that each creature can have peace and joy and love within them. He taught me how to find that inside of me.

Ralph's Poem

"I wrote my paper."

I told Ralph, the cat.

He stretches.

He says, "Raaalph."

He means, "Pay attention to Ralph...

The heck with your paper."

He stretches his paw

And touches my hand.

He rubs his chin

On the manuscript.

"I am real," he says.

"The paper...that's just words."

Purr Me a Story

Purr me a story, cat

Sing me your song

What do you do

All the day long?

Sit all morning

By the window pane

Watch the world

Go by again

Talk to the neighbors

As they go by

Pose quite nobly

Then catch some flies

In the afternoon

Take a long nap

Life's kind of easy

When you're a cat.

Rodney the Sheepdog

Will, this is a story about the largest of my pets, the Godzilla of my pets. Ask your dad, Aunt Cindy and Uncle Scott about Rodney. They will have stories. This is one of them.

Rodney the sheepdog was big and shaggy, a little clumsy, but very strong. He had big teeth and a very loud bark. This helped him in the job he had to do. He had to protect something. He had no sheep to protect. But, he had a family to protect. He had to protect Bill, Sally,

Christine, Billy, Scott, Cindy and Todd. And, he had to protect the house and the yard.

To do this job Rodney made sure there were no squirrels in his yard.

There were no rabbits in his yard.

There were no other dogs in his yard.

There were no cats in his yard.

There were no moles in his yard.

But, sometimes a bird flew over the yard.

There were no meter men in his yard.

There were no UPS men in his yard.

There were no newspaper boys in his yard.

Once a day the mailman came, but only to the mail box at the end of the driveway. Sometimes a school child would cross over the far corner of the yard and sometimes Rodney would allow this. Rodney worked hard at his job and Rodney did his job well.

One day Cindy came to her mother, Sally. She was going away to school. She had two rabbits that she needed Sally to take care of while she was gone.

The rabbit cages were set up in the breezeway. Sally brought Rodney to meet the rabbits in the cages. "Rabbits are our friends," she told Rodney. "Rabbits are our friends," she told Rodney at lunch time. "Rabbits are our friends," she told Rodney at snack time. "Rabbits are our friends," she told Rodney several more times that day.

The next morning Rodney was back at work.

There were no squirrels in the yard.

There were no other dogs in the yard.

There were no cats in the yard.

There were no moles in the yard.

There were no birds in the yard.

There were no meter men in the yard.

There were no UPS men in the yard.

There were no newspaper boys in the yard.

There were no school children in the yard.

But, there were rabbits everywhere.

Bill saw this and said, "What the …..?"

Sally said, "Rabbits are our friends."

Rodney the sheepdog had a job to do. He had a family to protect and a house and yard to protect and the rabbits to protect. Because Rodney knew that rabbits are our friends.

Now you know it too, Will.

Rodney

"Dishwashing's lonely,"

Rodney must think

He chooses that time

To come get a drink

Rattle a dish

Washer beware

Just turn around

Rodney is there

Brushing against you

Drools at your feet

Big, hairy dog

That once guarded sheep.

Tanka to Rodney

Rodney the sheepdog

Scratches at the bedroom door

Waking me each morning

With yelps and sloppy kisses

Before bounding down the stairs.

Chipper

It must have been the end of August, Anna. I was 10 or 11 years old. There was a pet show that year. I had the best pet ever. Chipper was a white rabbit with small patches of black on his ears. I loved him with all my heart. He was so cute. I was sure Chipper would win a first place blue ribbon.

The contest was later in the afternoon. First there were things to do to get ready. I fed Chipper his breakfast and talked to him about the ribbon we were going to win. I gave him fresh water. I cleaned out his cage and got him fresh straw. I let him out for a run in the orchard. He ran so fast, but I was always able to catch him. I must have been able to run fast back then too. The run is probably where I got patches of dirt on my arm and shins that day, and perhaps a skinned elbow when I brushed up too close to the cherry tree.

Finished with our run, I put Chipper back in his cage and went in for some breakfast and a game of gin rummy with my brother. I felt that he owed me a "win." Earlier that week we had been playing cowboys and indians. I had stumbled and he stood over me and pointed his toy gun at me. It had somehow dropped and hit me on the temple. It looked like I might have a permanent dimple there now. Anyway, he owed me. It was a good day so far. The game went back and forth, but I think I won the card game that day.

I decided to give Chipper a bath so he'd look shiny and clean for the pet show. He'd never had a bath before. I filled an old wash tub with water and got some shampoo. (I hope it was shampoo. My memory is not so clear on this. It may have been dish soap.) Chipper was surprised when I put him in the tub of water. He was even more surprised when I poured soap on him and scrubbed him all up. He was not pleased. He stomped his back foot splashing me, but had little choice but to put up with this indignation.

I rinsed Chipper off the best I could. I got a towel and fluffed him up. There were no blow driers in those days, Anna, so I had to let him air dry. Despite my vision and hope for a fluffy, clean bunny, he wasn't quite living up to my expectations. He was kind of scraggly. His hair was sticking up at odd angles everywhere. And, some of the hair had clumped up. I was sure Chipper would look better in time for the pet show. I put him back in his cage to finish drying off.

Chipper's attitude wasn't very good either. He was very grumpy. Perhaps a nap would improve his mood. Perhaps a bow would help.

With these thoughts on my mind, I went into the side yard. There was a baby squirrel  in the yard. It looked like it might have fallen from the tree. Her mother was up in the tree chattering squirrel talk, warning me to keep away.

Well, my grandpa was great with squirrels. So, I figured I would be too. Grandpa always had a pocket full of nuts. Squirrels would gather around him and he would feed them during his daily walks. I, of course, had a pocket full of nothing. Forgetting this minor detail, I just figured I could pick the baby squirrel up and put it back into the tree.

The squirrel had been through quite enough that morning. It had fallen. Her mother was scolding her. Now an awkward, half-grown human was trying to pick her up. The baby squirrel fought back and bit my thumb which started to bleed. Flailing, the baby squirrel was placed in the tree anyway.

I went in to tend to my wounded thumb. My last two attempts to improve the animal world were not working out so well. My thumb was throbbing but clean and no longer bleeding. I got dressed for the pet show.

Chipper was still kind of scraggly looking, but I combed and petted his fur down, picked him up and walked to the pet show. It was held at the elementary school two blocks from my house. We watched the judging of the dogs. A brown Labrador won first place. He could sit and he could roll over.

The cats could or would do no special tricks. But a fine white and black cat took the blue ribbon. I again figured Chipper was a sure winner.

We were in a catch-all type of category. If your pet was not a dog or a cat it was judged in this group. There was only one other entry in this category, a pet frog. It belonged to a snot-nosed, mop haired boy a few years younger than me. The frog was green. He sat there in the palm of the boy's hand. The frog's eyes were big and he looked around. But, he hardly moved.

Chipper lay in my arms and looked like...he looked like Chipper. He was a beautiful, fun and much loved bunny. I did not understand that the judges could not see through my loving eyes. They had to be impartial, I was told. They had to see through my rival's loving eyes too. The judges had to decide which the better pet was in this exotic, mismatched group. It was the judges' considered opinion that the blue ribbon should go to the frog. (the frog???)

Well, anyone could see that there is no comparison between a fat, green frog and my beautiful white rabbit. So, I took my rabbit and second place ribbon home, gave my rabbit an extra hug and a little more food that night. Anyone could see that a mistake had been made. My rabbit Chipper was the best pet around.

Weeds

"Go pull the weeds,"

She told the young girl.

"These are weeds. These are plants."

She went into the house, busy,

Never to be seen again.

The girl ate a rhubarb stalk.

Confused, the girl

First let the rabbit out.

The rabbit nibbled a few plants

Then ran. The chase was on. The rabbit

Was caught, secured, put in his home.

The girl turned back to the garden.

Now, which were weeds?

Which were plants? Hmmm.

It was later that she learned

During a dinner of meat and potatoes that, hmmm,

The plants were pulled, the weeds remained.

The girl cleared the table.

Sandy Dog

I was the smallest of the litter, but can humbly say that I was one of the smartest. I was lying with my brothers and sisters when they walked in. The small blond boy, barely out of babyhood, picked me up and cradled me. He and his mom brought me home.

I was named Sandy because Mom said I was the color of sand. As I grew, my hair turned into a copper color, but my Sandy name stuck.

I loved my new family and vowed to do all I could to protect them and keep them safe. The young boy, Todd, was fun and full of surprises. Once he hid a pig under his bed. It squealed all night and kept us all awake. All, except Mom. She somehow slept through it all.

Todd's big sister, Cindy, made sure I was fed and had fresh water. This was big brother Scott's job, but Cindy always made sure it got done. She had a good sense of order and routine. She helped with baths too when it was needed. And, she was great with girl talk and neighborhood gossip.

It was Scott who was the most fun. He snuck me treats. He took me on walks. He was always ready to play. He threw the ball for me and he threw the stick for me to fetch. Scott seemed to understand what I was thinking and what I was trying to say.

I slept in Todd's and Scott's bedroom. It was upstairs near the other bedrooms. I was safe, secure and loved. I was very happy with this family.

One night it was very hard to sleep. There were all kinds of scratching and skittering noises coming from the ceiling. This was a mystery. What was making the noise? This noise had never happened before, so if something had gotten above the ceiling, how had it gotten there? More important, when would it quiet down so we could sleep? I looked at the closet. Had something gotten into the closet, and then gotten into the ceiling? One of Todd's pigs?

The next morning Scott called, "Mom, something is in the attic. Something is making all kinds of noise over my bed."

She came into the room. Now that daylight had come, it was much quieter. She looked at the ceiling. Then she looked at Scott and Todd. She looked at the closet. Then she looked again at Scott and Todd and shrugged her shoulders. It was quiet. Whatever was making the noise had gone away.

"Breakfast will be ready soon," she said. "Get dressed and come downstairs."

So we ate breakfast and went on with the day. Scott and I joined the boy next door for a game of baseball.

That night the noise returned. Skittering and scurrying and scratching ghost sounds were in the attic. This time Mom heard it, but it was late and dark, so little could be done about it. I barked at the noise, but Mom and Scott told me to be quiet, so we did our best to go back to sleep.

The next morning after breakfast we went outside to look at the house outside the boy's bedroom. It was Cindy who spotted the small hole under the eaves. Had something gotten into the attic through that hole? Bats?

Mom shook her head as if she wasn't sure what to do. Who could she call for help?

The day went on. After some clean up we went to the park to play. Later, Todd and I were playing in the downstairs family room. There was the skittering noise again, this time in the walls of the basement! I looked at where the noise was coming from and barked. Todd thought I was playing and started chasing me and yelling. All of a sudden a squirrel joined us. It must have skittered down the wall and come out of a vent. Round and round we ran, and I barked and growled, hoping the squirrel would somehow run away. Clearly, it wasn't supposed to be here!

Todd slammed the door so the squirrel wouldn't get away. He slammed the door on my tail! I yelped in surprise and pain. The squirrel disappeared.

Mom came running down the stairs to see what all the noise was about. I wagged my tail, but it was bent and bleeding. Mom did her best to patch up the tail. Then she called Scott and Cindy and we all walked to the vet, about eight blocks away. This was in the days before Mom had a car. If we needed to go anywhere we had to walk.

I was in pain, but I was stoic. I needed to see the vet because I was hurt. The vet saw me right away. He gave me a shot so I could calm down. I really didn't mind. He cleaned my tail and bandaged it up.

I don't remember much about the walk home. I do remember being carried by Scott. He told me I fell down on the walk home.

I slept a lot that day. When I woke, the blood had been cleaned up in the family room, and someone had nailed a board over the hole outside the bedroom. Everyone fussed over me and they fed me treats. They said I was a hero who chased the squirrel away.

The next year when the raccoons came, I knew what to do. Protect the family and stay away from the door!

Pig Finding

By Todd Stelter

Age 4

One day I was vacuuming under the bed and I saw a pink pig.

The next day I looked under the bed for my shoes because I lost them, and I saw two pink pigs.

The third day I looked under the bed for my pet flea, and I saw three pink pigs. This went on until one day I saw fifty pink pigs.

The next day I looked under the bed, because I was playing hide-and-seek, and I saw a black pig.

On Friday I was looking for my art picture and I saw fifty black pigs and one white pig.....

I don't think I'll look under my bed anymore.

Christina

A Norse Folk Tale

Retold by Grandma Bliss

Once upon a time there was a widower who had a beautiful daughter named Christina. She was a hardworking girl, as all daughters of Norwegian descent are. One day the father said to his daughter, "This is your mother's locket. The time has come to try and sell it because the king's tax has come due."

"Of course, father," Christina said, for she loved her father very much, and cheerfully did whatever he asked.

As she walked to town, a small wren saw her and followed her. It was a long way to town and the bird decided to keep her company. "Here we go. I'll croon a tune as we go off to seek our fortune."

They soon came to a linden tree. The bird flew over it. Christina admired its heart shaped leaves and its pretty yellow flowers.

"Don't touch my leaves or pluck my flowers, and I will help you at another time," the tree said.

So Christina walked on, fingering the locket, and still smiling at the thought of the flowered tree. Soon Christina and the bird came to a dairy cow whose udder was very full of milk.

"Please milk me," the cow said. "I feel very heavy and uncomfortable. Drink as much as you like, then put the rest in a hollowed out log, and I will help you someday if the need ever arises."

So, Christina did as she was asked. The milk was sweet and good, and after she drank what she could, she put the rest of the milk in a hollowed out log and went on her way.

And then they came to a big sheep, shaggy and heavy with wool. "Please help me," the sheep said. "I am so hot under this wool. There is a scissors in the weeds. Clip my wool, take as much as you like, and leave the rest beside me. When you are in need of help one day, I will help you."

So, Christina clipped the sheep's wool, took what she could use, and left the rest beside the sheep. Then she went on her way.

Further on down the road, Christina came to an apple tree so full of apples that its branches were bent to the ground and even its main trunk was curved.

"Ohhh," the tree groaned. "Please pick my apples so I can straighten my branches and ease the ache in my curved trunk. Eat as many as you like, and lay the rest over my roots, and I will help you someday."

Christina picked all the apples she could until the branches were relieved of much of their burden. She ate a couple of the apples, shared one with the bird, and kept one for her father. Then she placed the rest of the apples around the roots of the tree and went on her way.

The path continued and Christina and the wren followed it a long, long way. It started to twist and turn this way and that way, but the girl kept following it. She was glad for the bird's song and company.

In time, Christina came to an old witch's house. It was dark and built low to the ground. She heard the wind hum low through the cracks in the wall. The girl had walked a long way, and she needed to stop and rest. Even though the house looked foreboding, she decided to ask if she could stay and rest for a while.

The bird was concerned. He knew the witch could be wicked, and could cause harm.

"At least hide your locket in your pocket," he told Christina. She removed the locket from her neck and tucked it deep in the pocket of her dress.

When the witch came to the door, Christina said, "I've been walking a long way and need to stop and rest a while."

"Well, what can you do for me if I let you stay here a while?" the witch asked.

"Perhaps I can do some work for you. And, if I do well, perhaps I can earn a little more to pay the king's tax." The girl said. "I can make a stone soup for a meal."

And then Christina went searching for what she needed to make the soup. She pulled out a large kettle, put a large, smooth, clean stone in it, filled the kettle with water, and added some onions, potatoes, carrots, beans, and some salt and pepper. Christina was careful to use only seasonings she was familiar with, because she knew the witch kept some roots and potions that had strange properties and powers. Soon, the kettle was simmering, and the witch and Christina had a fine soup for lunch.

The witch had to admit that the soup was good. This made her feel extremely uncomfortable because it nipped away at the meanness the witch had carefully nurtured within herself. This feeling was unusual and the witch did not like it.

"If you want to stay longer, you can stay in the barn," the witch groused. "But first you have to clean it out." The witch gave Christina a pitchfork to clean out the barn.

The pitchfork was big and clumsy to handle. Christina had trouble just picking it up. The bird saw her struggling with the pitchfork and found her a broom. "Take the broom, sweep out the barn, clean the room, come to no harm," he said helpfully.

The broom, indeed, was much easier to use. With the girl's deft touch, and using a bit of the magic the broom had in it, in no time at all the barn was swept out and set to order. The spiders saw this and decided not to build any new cobwebs during the girl's stay.

When the witch saw her barn cleaned out, she got very disturbed. The sense of order made her very uncomfortable. The witch was also concerned that perhaps her broom had been ruined, and that now the broom wouldn't do what the witch asked it to do.

"I have this black cape," the witch said. "It is old and has not been cleaned for a long time. Clean it and you will have earned your wages."

So, Christina cleaned the cape in a nearby river. Unfortunately, when she cleaned the cape, it turned white, which is not at all what the witch wanted. For everyone knows that when a cape turns white, it loses its evil magic and can only do good.

When the witch saw the cape, she knew she had to get the girl away from her and her home. But a deal was a deal. The girl had fed her, cleaned her barn and cleaned her cape as agreed upon, and so had earned her wages. "You've done the work well, too well. You have to go before all of my magic is ruined!"

The witch brought out three carved and painted wood boxes – a red one, a green one and a blue one. "Choose one for your wages for your work. And then go," the witch told Christina.

The bird whispered to the girl, "Don't take the green or red, filled with creatures and things you dread. Take the blue box instead."

So, Christina took the blue box and prepared to leave. The bird told her, "Hurry. Hurry. Be on your way. The witch will change her mind today."

Indeed, the witch was very angry at the way things had turned out. After a moment of thought, the witch decided she wanted the blue box back. She sent a magic arrow, a pot lid thrown like a discus, and a poison dart after the girl.

Christina hurried down the path, which luckily curved this way and that way, so the arrow, and then the discus, and then the poison dart missed her.

Finally, she reached the apple tree. The tree said, "Hide behind my trunk, girl. I'll spread out my branches to cover you. If the witch catches you, she'll hurt you and take the blue box from you."

So, Christina took the box and hid herself. The wren hid higher up in the tree. They had no sooner hidden themselves, when the witch came to the apple tree.

"Have you seen a young girl with a blue box come this way?" the witch asked the apple tree.

"Why yes, I have," the apple tree said. "She came by some time ago. If you hurry down the road, you may be able to catch her." The witch hurried on her way.

Knowing the witch was nearby, Christina ran to the sheep. "Come hide under my fleece," the sheep told the girl. "If that old witch catches you, she'll tear you to pieces and take away your pretty blue box." Christina crawled under the fleece and stayed very still.

Soon the witch came running up. "Have you seen a young girl on this path?" she asked the sheep.

"Ahhh, yes I did," the sheep said. "And Maam, she was faast. If you run baack that waay, you should soon catch her. Make haaste!"

So the witch turned back and ran the way the sheep had pointed out.

Next Christina ran to the cow. "Hide yourself behind the hollowed out log," the cow said. "If the witch catches you, she'll harm you and take the box. That would surely curdle my milk!" Christina did as the cow suggested.

Soon the witch ran up. "Have you seen a young girl come this way?" she asked the cow.

"Hmmmm. Soo, I did," said the cow. "Follow the road toward the mooon. You should catch her sooon. Mooo." With that, the witch ran down the road.

Next Christina came to the Linden tree. "Hide in my branches," the linden tree said. "If the witch catches you, she'll tear you to pieces and take the box away too."

So Christina hid in the branches. The little bird hid too. The tree spread out its branches with the yellow flowers and hid the girl completely.

The witch soon ran up to the tree. "Have you seen a young girl, carrying a blue box, pass this way?"

"Why no, I have not," the tree replied. "The day is so bright and beautiful, I'm sure I would have noticed if she came by."

The witch, completely discouraged, turned back towards her home.

When Christina returned to her father's home, she excitedly told him of her adventures. She pulled the locket out of her pocket and gave it back to her father for safe keeping. Then she showed him the blue box. They opened it and found all kinds of treasure within it. There was gold and jewelry, enough to pay the king's tax and more. They bought supplies for their pantry, shingles to repair their roof, and bird seed as a treat for the wren. And they lived happily and comfortably for some time to come.

Talking Cat

Emily, we need to learn to talk "cat."

One morning, Maya took me by the hand and led me to her food bowl. She stared dolefully at the bowl. It was empty, but the one next to it was full.

"Fill the empty one," she said. And, I understood what she meant, loud and clear.

Maya sat in the sunbeam, and cried woefully, "Play with me. Play with me before the sunbeam goes away. Play with me today. Isn't there a way you can make the sunbeam stay?"

One day recently, Maya licked my hand. Then she stuck her nose under my thumb and flipped my hand to her forehead. In this way, she told me she wanted her head petted.

Maya amazes me and astounds me. She's demanding, grumpy and pouty. But, I have learned some of her language. Sometimes I understand what she's saying and what she wants. I love that about her. She teaches me that all creatures have language, feelings and value.

Emily, we need to learn our pet's languages and tales. And, we can be the animal's friends. I believe the animals want to talk to us. Ralph surely did because he tried to imitate our language. Maya lets me know what she wants. So does Maggie in her own way. Sandy did her best to warn us of an intruder. And Rodney, well Rodney was able to understand what we were trying to tell him. Chipper, not so much. The young girl didn't know enough to listen. But, Chipper showed that he liked to run and didn't like his bath.

If we pay attention to the animals, sometimes we can figure out what they're trying to say. And, if we figure out what they're trying to say, we can be so much more than friends.

Maya

I thought you were chasing light

But you were chasing shadows

With all your body

With all your focus

You were joyful, quick and engaged

Chasing shadows away.

You look like a dancer

Balancing on light

Graceful and quick

Totally on point

Beautiful kitten

Lively and lithe

Now you're relaxing

Cleaning your fur

Stretching your body

Starting to purr

Sleeping, sometimes snoring

You are home, Maya girl.

About the Author

The author is a grandmother who wants to spend more time with her grandchildren. But, distance and time have presented some obstacles. So, she started to write memories of her pets, stories, fables, poems and bits of observation and whimsy to share with the children.

Grandma Bliss lives in Illinois with Grandpa Bliss and two calico cats.

Acknowledgements

I want to thank Pam Osbourne for all her encouragement and help in putting this book together. We spent hours discussing, planning and drinking coffee, as she patiently explained how to organize and piece the different parts of this book together. Plus, she made it a lot of fun! For her valued assistance I am ever so grateful.

Thank you Cindy Colin, my daughter and a writer in her own right, for your many suggestions. Thank you also for listening to my angst and frustration at getting the stories on to the page.

I am grateful to my pets who have left their paw prints on my heart. They have graced my life, shared their personalities with me and been there as life took its many ups and downs. As any pet owner can appreciate, I love each of them greatly. Thank you for sharing your stories.

And, to my long suffering husband, Art Woods, who can't quite comprehend why I want to clutter the house and our lives with all these papers and memories, thank you for your patience and understanding.

www.ingramcontent.com/pod-product-compliance
Lightning Source LLC
Chambersburg PA
CBHW051308170626
46809CB00004B/1796